LOVE CAKE

POEMS

Leah Lakshmi
Piepzna-Samarasinha

We acknowledge the support of the Canada Council for the Arts for our publishing program. We also acknowledge support from the Government of Ontario through the Ontario Arts Council.

Cover Art: *straining to reach the sun at world's end*, by Chamindika Wanduragala
Cover Design: Cynthia Griffioen
Author Photo: Alex Safron

Library and Archives Canada Cataloguing in Publication

Piepzna-Samarasinha, Leah Lakshmi, 1975-
    Love cake / by Leah Lakshmi Piepzna-Samarasinha.

Poems.
ISBN 978-1-894770-69-9

    I. Title.

PS8631.I46L69 2011   C811'.6   C2011-903256-2

Printed and bound in Canada by Coach House Printing

TSAR Publications
P. O. Box 6996, Station A
Toronto, Ontario M5W 1X7
Canada

www.tsarbooks.com

Acknowledgements

To the ancestors who bear me and speak through me, who have my back and push me forward.

To the family. Amir, Arti, Beena, Bruin, Chanelle, Cherry, Ching-In, Cooper, David, Fran, Hari, Karene, Laurie, Liz, Maceo, Manish, Mia, Minal, Nalo, Nico, Pike, Qwo-Li, Rabea, Sham-e-Ali, Stacey, Tiffany, Tre, Victor, Zakkiyah, Zavisha, for loving me beyond during the years these poems were written.

To all the lovers who blessed this door and bed.

To Amir, for coming back.

To Suheir, for breath, break, example.

To Sri Lanka, Toronto, Oakland, Brooklyn, Central Mass, where these poems were written and dreamed. To the Anishnabe, Missisauga, and Ohlone people, whose lands I lived on as I completed this work.

To movements that walk towards justice and healing, the end of abuse, and the creation of the safety we have never known and know deep inside. The gifts of INCITE, CARA, Safe Outside the System, Always a Safe Space, Revolution Starts At Home, Philly's Pissed and Philly Stands Up, UBUNTU, and generationFIVE. To all Sri Lankans who labour daily with our bodies, hearts, and dreams for justice and peace in our homeland. To the women of

I JUST came from a webinar: I will get into the program: I will win —

Equal Ground and the Women's Support Group for welcoming me home in 2006.

Mangos With Chili from now till infinity. June Jordan's Poetry for the People. Aya de Leon. Elmaz Abinader and Cristina Garcia. Suzanne del Mazo, Nicole Griffin, and everyone else who helped me survive Mills. Everyone who booked shows, everyone who got some use out of these words, everyone who gave some back, everyone who makes the art, life, family, and movements my eight and eighteen-year-old self needed and couldn't imagine and did. Sins Invalid for making the queer disabled artistic community of my dreams.

To my queer and trans of colour artistic elders, peers, and future.

Hekua hey Yansa. In my blood, a million stories.

Poems in *Love Cake* originally appeared in the anthologies *Some Poems by People I Like*, *Visible: A Femmethology*, *Ya Basta!*, *The Revolution Starts At Home: Confronting Intimate Violence in Activist Communities*, and the periodicals *Generations*, *Journal of Social Justice*, *Kartika*, *Left Turn*, *Make/Shift*, *Mizna*, *School*, and *No More Potlucks*.

11/17/2015

to the Black women on my campus, across campuses, the country, the world: I acknowledge you, I appreciate your gifts of conciousness, and I bear witness to your power. My ancestors — thank you — #BlackLivesMatter

Contents

coda: Sri Lanka, 2009

remyth

serendib

Class Notes 11/17/2015

☆ what can a poet do in times like these?

[Leah] WOCF INFLUENCES:

a career w/out Queer WOCF
for her is not possible —
vibrant, rich, yet invisible,
First Nations/Prisoners/
(Queer survival)
(alternative universe)
(our own cultural
(healing) reality)   La Gfrende's
                     Cnicke
My Life is Anchored) in
        survival .
              legitimitizing ↳

(tell the Truth)!! ①subrational
        ...   ❀ Suheir Mu
(Clifton)   ✣ poetry
  effective   people's
                         mawspaper
(Milk)
(VONA)
VOICES of Our
        Nation Junot
                 ☆RCU

after 31 years of loving in the war years
for the people of Lebanon and Sri Lanka, summer 2006

someday, habibti,
someday:

someday, our bodies are gonna tell everybody
just what it was like
to live through this

how the news ripped us open
morning and evening
crashed our sound barrier
shuddered our bodies
with bombs;

how we muttered place names
we knew intimate
as a punch to our gut:
your uncle's village,
the beach I have been told
is the most beautiful

how we took turns
watching each other watch Al Jazeera
muttering headlines that were inconsolable
how that time
you were the one to say
I'm sorry baby
I'm so sorry

how at night we dreamed war and sex

what you want out of it?
what credential
you want?

3

Pedagogy around healing that is queer + to run

war that rips us from our bodies
sex that brings us back *ung*

how we dreamed a day into the future
where our homelands are
dreamed what we couldn't know
had happened yet

how precious your belly's water was
under my hand
as precious as that last plastic bottle
to a family trapped five stories underground

how our bodies swallowed
everything
and they will tell
everyone
just   what it was like to live through this

because after 31 years
of loving in the war years
I think I should be better at this   I should be an expert at this
should know how to love
our way through this   fuck
our way through this
know how to kiss away every trauma

how 31 years into loving in these war years
I still don't know how to do this
but we cross this water together

still alive
still alive

4

dirty river girl

Central Mass grows crops of toughass girls
limestone and asbestos embedded in our hip switch
Takes a long time to walk miles of no-bus blocks ✓
so we grow impenetrable backs
screech tongues loud and obnoxious enuf
to shove five miles of *hey baybeeees* off our backs
and keep goin

Central Mass grows girls stolen 99 cent lipstick slick
eyes yearning   looking at 8 lanes of traffic
3 superhighways ripped out our city's heart
so everyone says oh yeah, *I've driven through there*
Grows girls who screw up our guts
and stick our thumbs out

wild like a forest
of trees busting through the abandoned train station
growing quiet for twenty years

Central Mass grows meth, crack and junk.
grows jails and youth lockup.
Grows an economy so busted you need a "connection" to get a
    job at Honey Farms.
Grows lead and asbestos. ovarian and cervical cancer at 27

grows the richness of abandoned. empty storefronts
endless sets of hearts lifting wings. abandoned warehouses
catch fire or fill with music. queers only 8 of us so we stick
    together.

that are
known as ther
" richness of
    abandoned"
silences many

Cambodia Puerto Rico Lebanon Black
and an army of half Irish-Polish half something browner girls
everyday like our white mamas' kitchen smell
our grandmas' empty margarine tubs✓

Worcester where working class section 8 folks buy 29-cent
    bottled water
cuz we got 7 hills of toxin. we an underground river bottled
    culvert waiting to bust open.
waiting for bioremediation
something cheap and unexpected
like human hair or old swap-meet clothes
soaking all the lead and PCBs out
to make something sweet   fresh
indisputably ours

rust belt all the way from Detroit
to Springfield. Lowell. New Bedj. Lynn Lynn City of Sin.
Woostah. Wormtown. Wartown. The Fart of the Commonwealth
Brick city in the eye of Cambridge. Northampton. Lexington.

I'm a set of broken hips tattooed with resilience
slick 99-cent lipstick lips
♭I start here
and go everywhere else.♯
- we must all

WOCF
claims/antiques

Sri Lankan resiliency miracle love poems 1–9

1.
Left our teardrop
we grow green chilis and curry leaf in balcony pots
in –35 degree
Toronto and Montreal winters. ✓

2.
When I flew the 27 hours home
for the first time at 31
I expected nothing
and the red earth just opened
right
up.

3.
Sneaking down the hallway
of the refugee Kennedy and Ellesmere highrise
to do it in the stairwell with the cute Jamaican boy next door
sleeping with your favourite cousin at the wedding
not getting married till late   or at all
and
you still love your folks
you still love you.

4.
Discovering you can make cutlets out of Bumble Bee tuna from
    the bodega
and ship Rainbow Sauce, good tea,

seeni sambol, Maldive fish, jaggary and hopper molds
to all the unlikely places in the world
where Sri Lankans be, including:
St Paul, Minnesota
Las Vegas   Connecticut doctor-lawyer town
and Thunder Bay, Ontario.

5.
Me learning how to cook Sri Lankan food at 23
from cookbooks in the library
taking a name researched in books
I don't know for sure is mine
but know for sure is not
the Dutch East India employee
who raped—I'm sorry, "married"
—my great-great-great-great-
grandmother
who
I know
is mine
unquestionably.

6.
Black August
chopped bodies
thick straight black hair burning
Smell of tropical meat rotting
and a thousand-year library in ashes. ✓

I am eight
I am in Worcester, Massachusetts
in my parents' backyard

playing behind the peeling white-planked garage
near the arbour vitas and the compost pile
reading tall stacks of library books in a hammock
a Lankan, a Tamil child
blessedly alive.

7.
Now that the island hemorrhaging
we need every drop of diaspora
all those pure bloodlines?
just rivers
mushy in the wetlands
jungle streams spilling down mountain to one sea.

8.
My grandmother's
bared ankles
her glare
straight at the camera eye
her mixed-race woman's
aching slit   fast legs
mango booty   running fast
in my body   I standing
her life   in mine
one   surviving   bombed out
lovely
palm tree.

9.
My father lost his tongue
but we make do with this one.

hurricane

When I wanted to call you lover in my language
I checked a dictionary out of the library
I couldn't afford to buy
traced the first ten vowels of alphabet
pasted them above my kitchen sink
repeated
kaykari   vegetable   *garappi*   uterus
nambu   trust   *ami*   turtle
azahahan   beautiful   *ahu*   become
munmunnal   before

It didn't work
so I took the bus to the subway to the RT
to the Tamil stripmall church named Miracle
walked to the back door
to give a bunch of tamarind-skin kids in hoodies
$15 for two weeks of language
plus free kottu rotty and pop

and afterwards I was eight years old, bouncing my butt on the
    bus
repeating my words: maran! a tree!
what kind of tree is it?
mamaran! a mango tree
I ask for the words for blood,
sister, love, lust,
get told without asking:
wetness, iram, go away, dog!,

deewali, my name
We joke about
how to say *he is a good son*
joke that every Lankan knows how to say
blood   memory

There's so many things you can do with your mouth
says the obviously queer speech pathology student
he says: stress the first syllable
put your tongue here
and here
all the way to the way back roof of the mouth
and I can say my name
I can imitate the aunties

Everyone says
Tamil's so hard, there's no way you can learn if you didn't
     growing up,
but the accent, there's 18 consonants and twelve vowels and one
     that is neither and
together they make 246 letters
and I want every one

I want this hurricane of syllables storming out of me
furious yellow butterflies beating in my throat
my teacher says
you can make any sound in the universe
with Tamil

once I wanted to call you lover in my language
the way habibti burst blood orange honey
on my shoulder

feminine firm of
"habibi"

11

I wanted kunju to come out my throat effortless
like it had always lived there   it has always lived there

now it does
I have the most beautiful words
curled up inside me

I took you with me

Dad, I was going to bring your ashes back
to the water you spent
your life trying to escape
You hated Sri Lanka
all the tight-assed people
who know three generations of your business
You wanted to fly away,
be from anywhere

You haven't died yet
so I took your letters to Colombo
so that even if you never made it
your words would
I thought I would open them here come back

like every second generation girl
who goes home
by the second week wants to go back to Brooklyn
feel normal   blend in to a mass of brown
where everyone's from somewhere else

and we sort of blend
sort of look out for each other
with our big dreams and bagels
high speed internet

America is the brain of the monster
You always said America was home now

now that you'd lived here for so many years
but did you ever feel like you had a home
except, like your daughter
anywhere there is coffee politics books

Dad, would you hate me if I brought your ashes home
or would you finally
finally
rest

for Agnes de Silva

did they stare at you as much as they do me
lady
not just as much   more
did you hold your head high
and learn not to give a fuck

grandma married at 32
to a last resort cousin
my lost appamına
whose stories hiss out between tight teeth
in this tight luscious island

as luscious as the eyes you met
the men and women you loved before marriage
burgher girls could flirt and become doctors, teachers
be hated
be wild
you frown just like I do

almost a century later
your daughter walks Galle Road
holds her head straight
bare ankles have become knees
the streets still hers to claim:
luscious   dirty   hers

appamma's ankles

I am my grandmother's ankles dancing
her smile of delight
her hair flapping in the wind
her limbs running free now

I ~~can't call your voice~~ back from the
~~transatlantic phone line~~
I've made you up
warrior woman
tough old bird
I've made you what I needed you to be
and what I dreamed
but I am your ankles dancing free now
your delight

you never smiled in any family photograph
not even when you saw me at birth and four
your life weighing heavy in forehead

I have the stories I stole of you
Black Jackie Alvis
of the Ceylon Labour Congress
Black Jackie of the union and the women's strike
Black Jackie Alvis almost ending up in Changee Prison

all the wild Alvis girls show their ankles, run fast
until they stopped you

you danced free once and now I do
I will be your ankles dancing free, ma
your delight

when you get a tattoo in Tamil

You sit for nine hours in an Oakland chair
praying they don't fuck up the lettering,
dissecting a breakup on your cell phone
while the needle burns colour into your skin.
Your radical aunties will never doubt you again:
one will tear her shirt open to show you the heart
with the blacked-out banner on her chest. My skin
may fade but this never will.

we smuggle spices

Multiple great-greats
of people who grew, sold, shipped, and cooked spice,
on our 28-hour long-haul flights home:

we slip curry leaf and Jaffna curry into our carry-ons,
arrack that's $4.90 in the supersave, not $50
Check No to Do You Have Fruits Vegetables Exotic Pets Animals
    box
The world's best tea two dollars, the supermarket brand is fine.

When the airport clerk tsks, pulls out a big cardboard box
and asks if we wouldn't rather mail it, shake no. Can't break this.
Careful save the empty Elephant ginger beer bottles to line
    windowsill.

In Parc X, a neighbourhood that, like Malcolm, has thrown off
    her slave name
saltfish rubs hips with sorrel, jeera, and rosewater. Marche Trinco.
On the last train out from the immigrant neighbourhood
we haul ripping grey plastic bags stretching home.

questions

did you ever memorize my name? did you figure out how to say
    it right?
did you find my country on any map? ask the temperature of
    the water?
watch me smashing ginger flat with the handle of a cleaver?
did you see the big plastic bags of red curry? ask the names of
    the poets of my country?
the hiphop? the baila?
ask me to describe the churning ocean's rage, the sound of plane
    wheels touching,
yellow rice 'n curry in tiny tin packages on the last plane home,
did you ask my grandmother's name, my father's,
what the bombs feel like there when they hit, did you ever kiss
    my toe hair
bless all the dark curls that fall out of the pick and wrap around
    the soap,
did you ever say when I said *do I look Sri Lankan today?*
baby, you look Sri Lankan every time I see you
                 every day
                 every time

unexpected

On the 28-hour Emirates flight to Sri Lanka
there are stars pinpricked on the ceiling
all the microwaved halal meals you can eat
and *High Fidelity* and *Armageddon* with the F-word beeped out

In Dubai I am the only
light skinned   high femme   hugely tattooed
four ripping bags   one pay-as-you-go cell phone
single at 32 with white creeping in my hair Lankan girl
at the gate to Sri Lankan Airways flight 471

And at the airport where my name is held on brown cardboard
after the The Punishment for Marijuana Is Death signs in three
    languages
after the brown parchment customs form with all the reasons to
    return but my own

I don't expect anything
I don't expect this to feel
familiar
or ancient
like not jinxing lotto tickets   completed job applications
    or crushes before you get 'em
I feel like I'm waiting for a nervous breakdown or a multiple
    orgasm
I feel the prayers of all my friends
like they're what's holding up the plane

I don't expect
this

brick-red dust coating kitten heels
pre-monsoon humidity curling my hair perfect
bucket baths
and 15-rupee string hoppers
and relatives who know how to drive drunk around all the army
    checkpoints
I don't expect
butches who are the Gay Games shot put champions of Sri
    Lanka
flirting with me by the outside toilets next to Miss Manuel
    Fernando's beach shack
genderqueer professors of English who teach lorde
my father's ghost-sucking cock behind the Bablapitya trainyard
    brushing me

the 300-rupee lunch packets
Nescafe and condensed milk
the sun leaving and returning to the earth at 6 am and pm
every day
every day
every day
I don't expect the infinite wisdom and patient resistance
of my creaky hipped aunties
arrack at the keels supersave
Mission Impossible badly dubbed in Sinhala
a closed A9 highway
children in white with perfect parts lined up for moments of
    silence
the screams of mothers watching soldiers beating sons
a sea that is a ghost
cupping 100,000 tsunami bodies
my dead uncle's name in cursive brown smoke in the kanaka

the sweet smell of crematoria flowers of a country
just another girl at noon under an umbrella
and *miss what are you*
is answered by
my father is Tamil
my mother is Irish
is not a surprise

$$\left(\begin{array}{l} \text{this home} \\ \text{is not a surprise} \\ \text{I} \\ \text{am not a surprise} \end{array} \right)$$

the kunju suite

rock

when we rock we rock earth to earth
belt buckle to pussy

our bodies prayers to keep us here
and when we pray we sing

there is this earth underneath it all
our cells spit molecules of home

when you say *I love you*
it's on purpose
when you say *I promise*
I believe you

grateful

grateful you gave me your naked back
grateful for your chest   no longer bomb crater
grateful that you cooked for me, looked out for me, didn't make
    me make all the first moves
grateful bombed out homelands understood through breath and
    sky
grateful your heart flew open under my hands

sitting on your floor, spilled sunlight, shelves of poetry, smoke
curling out Telegraph Avenue window.
dollar store tiara, queen girl. walking roses. cinnamon sugar dust
donuts and sun. skin kissed dusk. hand on thigh on subway. staring
down nasty men. tuberose vines that bloomed in a curtain may,
june, july, august out your window. never stopped blooming.

crisp warm jasmine flower. thighs brushing. spark.

the one who lit my cells up magic, not there. an absence pulled
    from side of me. bone broke.

I'm never not grateful.
                aren't we all?)
but I always want to heal things. community mama. excellent
    crisis counsellor. always finding the perfect word.

only this time I can't.

last night it was a steady cold rain. and I so wanted to take all
    my clothes off and lie on the roof with the rain beating down
    on my hurt.

26

*Las
afrenda*

steady there

now steady thump thump
hum thrum
of my heart
always there and still.

don't get me started

a woman's heart
blossoming out her mouth
a garbage disposal
of every horrible little thing.
the fat purple poison-headed blossoms
dripping over your city's freeway overpass
is my mouth. here
spitting poison bazooka over many hills.
my mouth drains lush,
my blood sluggish silt river
my mouth oozes
a woman's grief
machine-gun words
spitting, one
last song doesn't stop saying,
explaining, my woman's broken-hipped
plastic broken-doll body
ripped string
that talks and talks and talks

fuck me now fuck you

fuck me now fuck you now fuck me again!
oh boys and girls, girls and boys
there's nothing but trouble! nothing but
I don't fight other girls
and I don't want to fight you
and I don't want to fight
period, I am no good at it
and mama didn't raise me right
but I raised myself that way.
your body could start a war, already did
but I never wanted war with you
always wanted this bed to be where the oil
stopped burning, where we rested
lemon silk coverlet, your thick brown arms holding
—fuck me now fuck you now fuck me again!
your name flies beloved. your words pinpricks
of memory pricking me like stars in the sky. our tattoos flying
blue birds, plum candy flowers, the tikkural, a cacophony
of colour, blood, and beautiful scars,
fuck me no fuck you, no, fuck me again!—this is my
stupid heart, my open heart, my broken open heart
that bleeding, flying winged thing

when even I got sick of it I wrote a poem

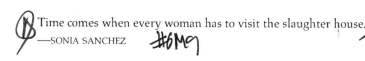

Time comes when every woman has to visit the slaughter house.
—SONIA SANCHEZ *#6M*

1.
this man ain't
Lebanon or Sri Lanka
I am not Lebanese dust although our colours matched up
and it'd be easier anywhere is easier than Sri Lanka
any house is easier to navigate when it ain't yours
any home simpler at a distance
this man ain't my only home the only home
I got the house I found I ran to

this man is the fantasy outrunning reality fast
this man is the toss-and-turn in my head
this man the worn-out bed won't allow me rest

2.
I'm bitter! Bitter bitter bitter!
All gurrrlllll, no he did not!
I don't care if she's a white Jewish girl from Argentina, she still
    don't got an ass!
You have an ass! I have an ass! It ain't even cuz she's white,
    why he gotta fuck with assless people!
Spending way too much time imagining taking that flower from
    behind her ear in the Myspace photo and stabbing her in the
    eye with it
some bullshit

about a woman I don't know shit about
whose heart is just as vulnerable to being broken
as mine
who I would bet money has been a sad queen like me
moody smoke staring out the window

3.
you know shit is bad
when you listen to the whole goddamn
Ani DiFranco breakup album
and sing along

4.
stud a three-quarter done jar
of honey with cardamom and cinnamon dust
take the train to the river
whisper *bless my heart momi*
tickle it free of this shit
let me build this house half-built
with some others
let it not collapse under one finger
one word

5.
wild woman in transit
wild woman face flushed
horny and mad
absolutely mad
can't stop talking about it
fuming cigarette, eyes wild

stabbing finger in the air:
and then he did this! And then ...
another crazy woman
talking to you in my head
talking to you on the subway
and streetcar and in bed
tiara breaking   grant denied
$68 of expensive makeup lost
towels stolen from the Y four years ago are threadbare
two eclipses and six planets in Scorpio and
Mercury in retrograde and you have my cell phone charger:
this is a fucked up
month

6.
when do I stop writing poems
as if you're still gonna read 'em
when do I stop writing poems
trying to measure up to yours
instead of this ragged sarcastic trombone of hips
swinging out   as I pour honey in a creek and whisper
turn my back   kiss this √
beautiful and fucked-up story goodbye

blue panties

throw my panties in the sea for Oshun   for you
wrap myself in cigarette ashes and grief
shroud me twisted in red sheets remembering
honey blood orange bursting juice on your altar
every moment   I felt heart behind your chest
breastplate   a kissful of gift
browngirl bedhead tangled with a loving's day after

pour our honey thick with ashes and wish
into the dirty river of the world
that pollutes our hearts
break   beat   break   beat
beat   my heart keeps travelling
grapevines unfurl on your shoulder
absent of me

all the mess of me
crumpled clothes dried sweat pussy on lace
this old sweatpant greasy-hair grief
vibrator on constant hum burning out
clicking memory beads on slideshow

boil my cock marbled red and black
tuck the photobooth pictures away
take our smiles off my altar
walk to throw blue silk panties into water
to she who has things planned for me
waiting in the ocean of tossing turning hearts

turn self
tend self
like I tended you
cherish
tender
wish
aqua scarf fluttering

what is left

in transit

1.
1943   my mother is too poor for real doctor for polio
public hospital doctor tells her parents: buy her a bicycle
if she moves her hips enough, maybe the nerves won't seize up
each day escaping drunk daddy/shouts hitting/a house that does
    not love
skinny bespectacled smart girls/she pushes her bike to the end
    of the driveway
whispers *left? or right?*
cracked grin on her face
all pleasure, all freedom
between her legs as she steps out
and pushes off

2.
at the dawn of time when my mother's hand slips
fondles me to shut me up
and I split into atomic particles hovering
a cloud over tiny girl body
that will stay away for two decades
she is split too
my white mama
who took me to the library
and brushed my hair straight till my scalp bled
forbade closed doors and walks off the block
and loved

at 16 she forbids friends and driver's license
at 21 in college calls every day
at 22 I get on a Greyhound bus with two backpacks,
and leave her and everything that is America
At 22.5 I send her a letter
and do not pick up my phone

At 23 my fibro shaky hips and butterfly quiver mount an adult
    tricycle
the bike you can't ever fall off
At 32, I learn to drive
and pilot an early '90s Toyota
through streets filled with people who look like me
who would terrify her
my thighs strongshifting easy
all freedom   all pleasure between my legs
as I whisper *left*   *or right?*

the best daughter

I'm 22 years old
and my mother doesn't know where I live!
I'm 33 years old
and my mother doesn't know where I live

It's a happy song
a happy little song in my chest:

I am the worst daughter in the world
and the best
I do not visit   I will not change
my mother's diapers when she is old
and I will not molest my daughter
the way she did me

I am not the passive voice
Even as a small child
thundercloud blackpurplegold snarlopening
my baby vulva stretched and split
my voice is speaking

My memories are not false. They are mine
Bathroom floor downstairs,
I'm six and all of a sudden
I feel my baby vulva in mine
tiny and pink   the feeling is pink   bud
touched and bad

the baby feeling. the terror in my eyes in every family
    photograph.

the secret language. the escape hatch out the top my skull to the
    pine trees:
all these are real. I submit them as evidence in the court of true
    justice
that hasn't shown up yet
As admissible as any videotape
I my own expert witness

I know that when my mother touched me
I not alone
children boys girls and children both and neither
were being touched by their mamas daddies aunties grandpas
    right at that moment
terrifying monsters   best beloved

I climb. My survival is written in the stars
in the stalls of the Salem Square library branch in the 1980s
in the two old growth pines behind my house
in all the books I read about children
who ran away. the suitcase packed since 7. the orgasms I learned
    how to have. honey dust on every lover's pillow. every single
    second I stayed inside my body.
my story was everywhere. it was smeared in the pine trees, at
    CVS, every seat on the Chinatown bus, every cheap plane
    ticket.

when my mother touched my genitals,
she was a ripped-in-half, frightened raging girl
she was a thirty-seven-year-old woman
she did evil
she was my mother
split open, flying

my mother is still alive
and so am I
and so am I

vico'd out in the house they finally paid off
she doesn't know where I live
and where I live is a house with sari-coloured walls open to the
   sky
a big red bed spilling books
and all the windows open
A door I open
and close

the worst daughter
and the best
my child's heart lifting hope to sky
that she blesses that I made it
finally off South Flagg Street
finally back in my body
finally all the windows of the house
wide open
and safe

grace

I am sitting at my desk.
Lift coffee, look out wide window. Sunlight, hot lavender flowers
sweet and musk, deep plum centres. I am thirty. I close my eyes,
I am twenty-two, it's July, 1997. I am clutching on to the side of
    a van
going ninety, my father is screaming

as he goes 90, 100, 120 miles an hour down a two-lane highway
After the fourth hour I'm crying like I'm eight
as quiet as I can in the back seat.
My mother whips her head around once
hisses *what's wrong with you?* shrugs away before I can answer.

When we pull up to my new house
he jumps to hurtle out boxes, dimple snarling.
I walk slow to my front door
All the fear has been burned out of me,

all the feeling
When he slams up my front steps, I put up my hand
Say
This is my house. You can't talk like that in my house.
He looks like he wants to punch me in the face, but won't,
like he has forever.
He turns and goes around the corner where the house leans
    peach, wild tree.
My mother says *what have you done to upset your father?*
When I went home, the first one

that wasn't one, no ghosts came up to me on the streets
I looked everywhere for my father's face
but didn't find it.
My memories didn't sit beside me on the bus
they were in my head, in history.
This was just a city
where eight years had happened while I was gone.

All the history filled my body, scanning the cars for fear
that a tall iron grey man would be in them
sad with my eyes, with my history rotting in his hands and
    teeth
I thought he might not recognize me in a cackle of fluttering girl
    birds
that he might not know me happy
that he might not know his daughter with her hips flying
her hair floating. That

the grace of running, the grace of empty rooms
and changed phone numbers
the grace of love that had not touched him and my mother
had touched my face once and changed it so much
he would never recognize me again, his only daughter

that after their hands had stooped my spirit
the angel of runaways had touched me that day and said *go*
and said *once you do*
he will never know who you are again.
They will not say your new name, they will not be proud of
    your new face
but you will be free
Your new face circled in flames

the wind singing your name with joy
a blessing that day, that grace
that brings me here to windows,
hot pink and plum musk flowers

thirty, unbroken by my history
walking in a new city
my body waking up singing
every day from that touch

when your parents made you

When your parents make you, it is Chile, 1974
They think they will raise you in a revolutionary sunlight
but you are born in a refugee camp to a mother alone
as your father sits in Pinochet's prison.

When you show me the one photograph of your childhood that
    exists
you are four
Your delicate fro spreads like sunrise
as your wide-open eyes stare away, fully disassociated
At the immigrant kitchen table
your mother rocks thick black eyeliner and wings of hair
holding a cigarette over a smile insisting
She looks like her hummingbird heart is about to explode
Your father grips her heart
like a cigarette between his fingers
He is the one about to explode
Your heart flies off someplace else.

At fourteen you run away from them
sleep on couches and stairways
spray TORONTO IS HUNGRY everywhere
When the LA rebellion explodes for your birthday
you smash all the windows of the McDonald's
and make the front page of the newspaper
You cross the border in the trunk of a car.

You hitch to LA
where the national guard is still on the sidewalk

Your eyes are still somewhere else
as you beat up skinheads,
throw some off a roof
get trailed by for years by that one cop
You soak stamps in rubbing alcohol delicate
write letters longhand to prisoners
walk across the city on one falafel.

We have sex the first night
after watching *Brother from Another Planet* on video
I am trying to look like a South Asian Kathleen Cleaver
You have two pairs of baggy pants and one twin futon mattress
You have the Angry Brigade and *The Wretched of the Earth* in
    your bookcase
We tag *Pepita and Chanchito 97* on the walls of the underpass
The security guards tell us to stop kissing in the lobby.

You pull out your knife as we try to have sex in the playground
when a man jumps out with his dick in hand
You tell me you've always wanted to die
but feed me, give me books
I've never been this happy.

I pull you back from the window,
jam my shoulder in the door
to the room where you're trying to cut your wrists with a pink
    daisy razor

Everyone has thought you were crazy for so long
you're bi, talk about abuse, being crazy
Being lightskinned tortures you
like an itch that never once stops
You try to rip your eyeballs out of their sockets

because you think they're blue
You sneer, *at least when they think you're white they think
     you're Italian.*

I meet your mother and she and your dad take us out
before the food comes you and your dad are circling each other
     in the street
Go on, hit your old man
this is why you left
but almost ten years later you want your parents
You start to say that, after all
your father was driving a cab all night
working another job during the day, going back to school
to learn what he already knew
on papers the government declares useless
You start to treat me like he treated you.

Eyes disassociated but fixed on something else
Years pass, I leave
I can't make your eyes focus
I can't stop the relentless step of the
skinheads and fathers and fists
in your head.

You always said you would go crazy if I told these stories
that you'd go to the cop shop and kill as many as you could
but this is my story I'm telling, not yours
my story of where violence comes from
where it goes.
You tell your own story I hear secondhand
where you say you just slapped me once, it wasn't that bad
Me sweetheart,
I tell a different story.

irresistible

I close my eyes
see the corner of Queen and Lansdowne
where we fell in love
just outside Ali's Roti Shop
where you backed me into a lamppost and kissed me
biked off with a shit eating grin and my lipstick
all over your face

Generations of our parents made home here
in these hardcore cockroach Jameson apartments
Jaffna curry in our bellies
browning Polaroids of backhome

I had your head in my lap so many afternoons
eating $2.99 eggs and coffee at the Tennessee
ripped couches fixed with duct tape
like my uncle's house
until one day the sign was down
newspaper covering the windows
Landmarks fell irresistible to wrecking balls and galleries
like rotting teeth
pulled because welfare wouldn't pay for filling
they cashed in on this beauty we danced outta nothing
till I couldn't recognize my home

If we didn't have Sri Lanka
at least we should have this
these small ten blocks of city

but they make us pack up and leave
every generation
till the idea of a village is impossible
the idea of being from anywhere
for 300 years
ridiculous

this land we made ours
with every tired step home from the subway
every breath of smog and ashes:

some things can't be measured in money
Railroad tracks and empty lots
are where cities go to dream
You and me
each others home
dream oceans   the smell of Jaffna curry and old
   photographs.

this is where it felt like the streets buzzed so hard
they might just crack and rise from the concrete and float

we're overdrawn and in love

I spend my tax refund buying you an expensive leather slapper.
I buy panties and flowers, miniskirts and stockings.
I rack up my credit card, I buy a corset.
Wash my slips in white flowers and sugar water.
Show up at your door after your daughter is asleep.
Meet you naked in your twin bed
you bought when you thought you wouldn't have lovers,
your chest's centre
is better than. And I say fuck debt, fuck overdraft
fuck 13.9% interest and my FICO score,
let's buy $150 of fruit at berkeley bowl.
let's buy out the taco truck
bounce the rent cheque.
You are better and more important than what
I'll owe Mastercard when I die.

this is what it looks like
when it finally comes

I open under her hand
wider than I ever have
and there's no clenched fist vulva, no bleeding,
no little welts rising up on my labia saying no
I open to her fist like the biggest cracked grin
bigger than anything I've known how to know

this is what it looks like
when it finally comes:
I'm not divided
halfway down my body
the part cowering in bed for days
and the part flying cigarette legged rapid tart smack:

my hips are not broken. they shake during yoga and I stroke
   them
others shake too. I take that girl out of the closet.
There's nothing in there for her.
I unpack her. show her

I never have to go back to that light blue
maple-shaded girlhood room
my bed is warm, red-honey-poured, and sunlit
pillows plumped coo: rest, rest
finally enough rest

there is finally enough
she is finally enough
I am finally enough

this is when I am no longer girl and always girl
this is where I am 33 years old
and it finally came
red-honey-plumped hips
cooing rest, rest
flying more than I ever knew how to know
wide like the biggest cracked grin

sweetest thing/tierra sagrada

1.

I have an ongoing thesis about brown people loving brown people and brown people loving white people. It's an unfinished one with lots of unproven hypotheses. I need to gather more raw data to evaluate, but there are times when the scientific method breaks down and is inadequate to describe what goes on in my pussy and my heart.

But this is what I know. Sometimes it's the sweetest thing. Sometimes, its boredom and bullshit. Sometimes I will open my legs and give up my head, heart, and panties to the sky based on nothing more than skin that is the same colour as mine and lips as full, that can say my name right or at least make a stab at it. I'll forgive them if they fuck it up if at least they try hard at it. I'll forgive them so much. I need so bad to be forgiven.

I want to fuck them back to before. before before. before the ships arrived on our lands, before our white parents fingers probing genitals, hair and skin looking for marks of the devil, before the breakups with each other like earthquakes we never expected that threw carefully arranged plants, plates and books to the floor of the room. I want the fingers inside their holes to dry erase their scars the way theirs did to mine. I want it to be precious. I want it to be private. I want to be fearless.

There are certain things you just don't do, certain things you just don't tell anybody. Not family business that should be shared, but certain things secret like a cervix or that crinkled place that cries in my cunt. Like how I never talk about my spiritual beliefs despite the altar that has taken up a quarter of my room since I turned 18 and got a room of my own. I don't trust people who run their mouths 'bout Yemaya or their pagan healing circle. The gods don't talk to people who talk about them too much. You get down on your knees to her in private and she gives you things, that's how it works.

And there are certain things you don't give white people is what
    I've thought
I am a nationalist!
I mean it!
I mean
I may fuck you when there is a shortage but I won't hold your
    hand in public!
I won't cook you Sri Lankan food
call you kunju
make my culture a Disneyland road map for you
There's certain shit that's our secret
I had to work hard enough to find it
and I'm holding on to it
like our ancestors held on to the location of Palmares
like that last apartment where the Tamil woman activist is
    holing up from the cops and the LTTE
like the last bit of rez cupped hard
There's certain things you don't ever give up to whitefolks
no matter how much you might love them
no matter how idiotic some of our own might be

There are so few of us
and like Chrystos said, that's why we don't fuck sometimes

because there are so few of us
because friendship is safer and lasts

but for a year
I fucked my peer group
and nothing was sweeter on my tongue
nothing was sweeter than those excerpts of my magic fuck life

2.
I usedta have a rhyme with that one lover, like:

white boys are like fast food
well advertised
a lot has gone into making them taste good
sometimes there's nothing else on the side of the highway
but your tummy sure does feel funny after
white girls are different!
sometimes they're like fast food too
sometimes they're a vegan hippie salad!
sometimes they're fatback   biscuits and gravy

sometimes brown people fall in love with us on the first date
give us a UTI cuz they're banging your pelvic bone so hard
or just ain't it

but sometimes
sometimes . . .

3.
I know how high stakes this love is. And I know I haven't wanted
to be fed anything else but dynamite. Nothing but brownness like

sweet chai and paan chewed and sipped on the sidewalk under Christmas lights, sold by an uncle with a card table when it is oh so cold.

Basically it is Arabs and Latinos and the occasional South Asian and any kind of mixed person who wants to do it with me. And then of course there are the white geeky post-anarchist guys who used to hate me and later loved me and wanted to fuck me because white anarchist boys always want to fuck angry brown girls as a complement to their bell hooks collection. I am an ex-punk who hated it who now likes to sometimes walk through those group houses aloof. I used to make white guys give me head for nineteen hours as some form of *reparations, beyatch!* for colonialism.

And then I got over it. Brownness was a relief. The biggest exhale.

4.
Sometimes the queer community of colour is so small. so wanted. so necessary. so drama-filled. so exhaustion-ridden. I know everyone's secrets and keep them safe. I have boundaries, I have rules. That there is no room to move into the spaces that I so desperately want.

I don't know how the story ends. I am still gathering data. I know love never stops seeing colour. I know love is an anarchic bitch that will slap your ass and upside your head and send you places you'd never thought you'd go.

palms full of Oshun

1.
no more smoke and ashes
honey welling up
the center of my palms

2.
yes I'm an affirmative action dater
but why would I spit in Oshun's face?
that would be really, really stupid
don't you think?

all my prayers to Oshun are like this

all my prayers to Oshun start off like this:

Momi, I don't want to bug you because I know folks always be bugging you. like how Maceo would call me and say, "every time I pray to Oshun lately, she just yawns." I just want you to know that I really am grateful. I am grateful for the lovers who have showed up when they were supposed to, even when the way some of them left is not how I would've wanted them to. I am grateful for the gigs that pay real live green money and the pretty clothes and the everyday pleasures, walking through the farmer's market under rain wet leaves, my thighs brushing. all that Taurus-ass pleasure shit, good food and H&M earrings and baths and friends and wine. all the people who love me. all the shit you showed me this fall and winter and spring when the bottom fell outta the magic wave, when you were waving your hands in front of my face yelling see! love is not just that boy. love is all this shit. I'm real smart but real slow sometimes but always I am really fast and I want things to come fast. thank you for being so generous with throwing shit at me till I got it. I get it. I am grateful.

at Blockorama this year there were nine thousand black and brown queers dancing in the parking lot of the beer store. the party got moved to Church Street which had the advantage of making more of a Black queer presence on the main gay strip, but the lot was a lot smaller and it also sort of felt like being in a cage. a woman went into labour backstage and another woman had a seizure. and then coz came on and spun the most incredible forty-minute remix of a hymn to Yemaya and everybody was just going crazy.

dancing the way I like to dance and have a hard time sometimes getting to, no worry about whether I have rhythm or look cool or look like a fool, just going nuts and dancing hard and fast, giving it up. me and Melinda swirled our skirts and danced hard and I closed my eyes and prayed.

all my prayers to Oshun start off with me going on and on about how I am so grateful for all the shit I am grateful for, that when I get to the end of it, I forget what I was gonna ask for. I forget what the but was.

the but is *but there's a place in my pussy my arms aren't long enough to reach. there's a spot on the back of my neck I can't kiss by myself. so momi, I am grateful, but if you could see your way of throwing me some really good magic fuck boy or girl sometime soon, I would buy you flowers and chocolates.*

I would smear flower petals and dark chocolate bitter and rich all over my sheets and crusting into my body's creases. I would have rain water trickling down my leg and rub up against some tree bark. I would make a list of things I want to do. I would cherish the smell of lying wrapped up in another rising from my bed and honey crease knees. there would be gold glitter and cupcake crumbs dusted in the crease of her knees, petals cupped secret in the centre of my palms.

I thank you for the pretty ones who show up at the bathhouse and friend's going-away parties and become a good story, a good moment, where I bike away standing up yelling thank you, where my ass sets the fire extinguisher off and it floods the hallway, where she kisses my heart and says thank you and I say it back. I would buy flowers and chocolate, enjoy every moment, not fall

so hard so fast, go home to my own apartment. have a two-night
-a-week rule, not be scared to dance, not be scared to be dork.

the thing about fucking family is they heartbreak out like family except family you had real good get down with. or they can be that cousin you got drunk with but had the big falling out with and don't talk to for years, and then maybe you do or maybe they get in a car crash and it's just like that. the thing about family is you need them and you survive the loss of them anyway. like how sherman alexie said that he loved his wife but she's been around eight people since they got married and he'd liked around five of them.

anyway, I prayed to Oshun and stomped and got coated with sweat and smog and a woman went into labour backstage. and I keep feeling how I'm not running from anything any more, I'm just deciding where I want to show up next.

lucky

when I get a butch or a boi in my sights
I know I have to talk fast and perfect and smooth and real
to get my hand inside you
all the way to the wrist.

on my 34th birthday I get the word lucky tattooed on my right
wrist.
I get it so that every time I write, wipe piss off my pussy, or turn
the page of a book
I am reminded that I am indeed lucky.

I didn't choke to death on the umbilical cord wrapped three times
around my neck when I was born.
I didn't get killed by either of the truly dangerous men I married
at 19 or 23. I didn't kill myself at 11 or 12 or 18 or 18 or 22 or last
week. I might've left this body for two-thirds of my life but I came
back into it through my left armpit. I am here and here and here.
I have only been evicted once. I am not trapped in bed or in a
marriage or a jail cell or a nursing home.

I'm lucky and when I get in my sights, in my bed, I whisper, "I
know that you're not any gender you don't want to be just because
you let me inside you." trust me with your breaking and your
whole. let me stroke your cock from the inside. when leslie
feinberg wrote that if you put your cock inside someone you can
either make them feel better than they've ever felt in their life or
remind them of all the ways they've been hurt, I listened.

I'm a femme who bottoms and I know this as the opposite of

worthless. teaching yourself to respond. receive bear witness wince give it up and take it be my boy my girl my blessing. I am so lucky to get it. you are so lucky to get it too.

the war's on and the rents high. but we have five minutes. a kitchen table. this breaking of skin. let's take this. let me feed you anything you can be fed.

SBBFF4EVA
(Slutty Brown Best Femme Friend 4 Eva)

girl your cleavage is all I need to rest my head on
you will drunk drive me home anywhere

you a 2 a.m. open all night halal sweet shop
run by immigrant uncles
who in my dream smile tender at our hoochieness
your words a full pastry case spilling full of every kind of
     mirthi   jamun
you enough $5 Salaam phone cards to call home anywhere

sophisticated in multiple brownness
you cup my colour in your cleavage
say that I indisputably brown despite white mama
because I
     a) wear bangles every goddamn day, even with booty shorts
          and
     b) have no problem shrieking in the street

your belly
strong brown tea
lotsa milk
lotsa sugar
shippable across worlds

you give the best damn
post abortion massage
brave your belly
answering craigslist ads
following the words

insisting on colour
finding your brown femme god in Ross Dress for Less
and god damn she looks like you:
a magenta sequin floorlength prom dress with corset back
on the clearance rack
for $12.99.
you call me back
every
damn
time

TD Visa customer #209802929

8:00 a.m. and everything on the front page of the *New York*
    Times
is all bold all capital second week in a row
I pick up the copy slapped outside our apartment door
pad to my backyard
water yellow pear tomatoes and drying-up cosmos
I hope will be enough to feed me.

8:00 a.m. and it's my regularly scheduled wake-up call
1-888-625-8890
or the more creepy "ID withheld"
that sets my stomach plunging
my thumb hits Reject without thinking
I don't pick up voicemail for a few days
because messages saying, "This is an urgent call from TD
    Canada Trust"
or even worse, *robots* calling me wanting to know where my
    Visa payment is
freak me out
I want to know where it is, too
I tell myself that Merrill Lynch can't pay their bills either
so why the hell should I worry about Mastercard, Visa, and the
    $16,000 line of credit
that nice desi gay boy who liked my accessories gave me at
    prime
when he really shouldn't have.
Try to keep my chin up
tell myself that it's okay to bounce the rent cheque

buy a $4 sour cherry icecream with a kiss of dark chocolate in
the tip
that plenty of the best people have horrible credit.

My people know how to hustle
I grew up listening to my mother lie
to the phone company and the oil man on the phone
her voice getting tighter, whiter
like we had thousands of dollars lying around
and were just a little careless.
The sky is falling, I can't afford gas
I scroll through my Metro PCS phone
seeing friends' names with *unemployed*   *chronic*
*illness with no insurance   just lost disability   in nursing
school with no student aid* written in ghost dust on their faces
and wonder if I should be looking for free chickens on Craigslist
planting grain.

I'm a 33-year-old woman with four jobs
$37 in my chequing account
plenty friends, books and glittery body products
looking over my shoulder back twenty years
to my mother's three jobs and no divorce
so she can keep the house.

The men on the front page of the *Times* look freaked the fuck
out
but the sky has been falling for a while.
Apocalypse just ain't enough to scare us
cuz we've lived through a few already
and that   maybe
is the point.

no matter

no matter how broke
immigrant   off the books
non-paid   non-heated
four months behind on the rent grey wall-to-wall apartment
$37 in an empty yogurt container in the fridge
your life has been
you've always fed yourself
and had at least one pretty dress

your bruises washed off
one good friend who'd bring you oranges
backyard dandelions for greens
tincture from cheap vodka and burdock root clearing your liver
a junkpicked plum futon to lie on
and dream   dream

no matter how sick you get there's always the time
when the fever breaks   you rise from old sweatpants
and head to the shower
there is plum eyelid glitter
and gold dust winging your nipples

no matter how uncertain the stakes for a
queerbrownladypoet
with no parents' wealth waiting
you pay the rent
fill the sink with dahlias
have time to sing

femmes are film stars

Femmes are film stars
in the movies of our lives
Instead of dishwater we choose danger
grab belt buckles, smooth lip gloss
and make eye contact
we put Bollywood to shame

we're the stars of our own danger-filled whirlwind
there are dramatic plot twists and more edge-of-the seat
    moments
than you can believe
and suspensions of disbelief?
girl, you know we suspend disbelief
do shit ain't nobody supposed to be able to pull off
we're our own romantic epic
like Frida in Paris
Audre in Mexico
standing on two tree trunk thighs
planted firm and swishing

when we were girls and someone said *diva*
we breathed in that word
and it turned into a glimpse of a woman we saw once
on a multiplex screen
a beautiful lady
who shone in her skin
and rose out of it
maybe it was our favourite aunty

or our mama when she was young
maybe it was Frida or Rosario
maybe we've never seen the one that could be us yet
but we make her up
we make her up outta thin air
outta brilliance and ass

it's not always so glamorous close up
there's a lot of shit in making movies you don't see
I mean sure there's
vintage slips
booty shorts
fabulous moments

but backstage
sometimes it's a little more complicated
you're the director *and* the producer
you gotta figure out
how to walk down the street   how much skin you
    want to show
how to fuck in the middle of the club   how to feel it
how to get a discount on the copies   get immigration
    status
not get deported when the club is raided   not get kicked outta
    the organization

and even though this is a movie
it's the kind Hollywood will not make
we'll go to *Josie and the Pussycats* just to see Rosario Dawson
sit through *She Hate Me* for five minutes of Sarita Choudhury
but we want more than that for our children

so we make our own movie
as we walk down the street
make revolutions with chipped turquoise nails
spread thighs and hard cocks
eight hours goooood sleep and dreams on satin wishbone pillows

and dreams?
girl, when we dream
we dream
the cliffhanger ending
where girl is never bruised
spread thighs never despised
where every girl
can be the star of her own glitter-dusted revolution

we dream the place
where our lives
are what girls get to grow up
to be

my hips are wings

the years pile up
longer than I ever thought possible
30 years after white mama fingers
15 years after moving out her house
13 years after turning around and saying, "okay, what?" to
    trauma
9 years after never speaking to them again
2 backpacks on the Greyhound back to myself
12 years after reading Chrystos and Sapphire standing up in the
    bookstore
10 years walking back inside my breastbone
5 pretty bras   6 years of a door I could lock against
    anyone
4 years no fucking   3 years brown girl yoga
no personal trainer except the universe
books   friends   space   prayer   la diosa
Kali smacking my ass into something new
and I am not the same
I am not the same woman
I am not the woman I coulda been
just the miracle I made myself be

I don't rise out my body anymore . . .
I rise out of it
spirit crowning as I pump your ass
as you flip me on the bed
as I hiss *lick right there*
as your chai belly   platano thighs

perfect hands meet mine
make miracle home on this bed
big boots   girl curls   brave
I never leave my body any more
I
am
right
here

ayesh, nablus

a found poem
Democracy Now, January 12, 2009

no place of refuge
under a murderous phosphorous white sky

no place.
no place untouched

a tender kiss, a waltz good-bye. of ambulances screaming and
    running out of gas
of brothers buried on top of sisters. of eight square miles of
    hosed-down blood
of

nowhere safe. or sacred
everywhere safe. or sacred.

be numb or fight. which is better. I don't know.

Mahmoud

in a memory wide and deep as the sea
there are children walking on water on the path of sun's light
the one that's all lit up. your children float
on the salt of your words
you are dust of
Palestine, Q'ana miracle, soil embedded
in each of your ashes flying.

voice of your people, you shy of world.
now gone,
we eat lentils and onions, dip pita in zataar
before a Noe Valley altar flying for you.
cup head that might turn to brain tumour of beloved.
in San Francisco by a bay blue and white and gritty as your
     home town,
Amir reads your poems to a cute gay boy from the mosque
and his hulking bear boyfriend in a Castro café.

we cook lentils. cup head of beloved to breast. speak your words
     held aloft on
altar of body. you gone to ultimate freedom
your words stuffed in pocket   slipped on carry on luggage
     without fee

the work of a poet: to document, to sing
to remember, insist
to incite, to call: peace, peace
I have read your poems to my beloved on AC transit
I have declared them a burnt gold sun behind forehead
I have insisted on the precise blue of sky, the endless waves

        licked by flame
I have insisted on all words and colour available
I have insisted on memory

who will I be when I become the poet
who will we be, us who become you

to each country its war
to each war its poet
to each poet a death
scattering words like seeds

you say Oakland reminds you of Lebanon

close your eyes enough
and you could almost be home
the hills you lift eye to
white stucco building birds coating the hillside
always the water and blue sky horizon

Toronto reminds me of Colombo:
little fucked-up buildings
no-count people
Sri Lankan West Indian East Indian Caribbean Canadian
    Groceries
phone cards and rotting mangoes
we buy minutes home for a dollar each.
guys hanging outside Little Burma all night
smoking cigarettes even worse for you than the regular kind
condoms for a quarter   two loosies for a dollar
a pack of Native for two
but there is never any milk

Toronto reminds me of Colombo
skinny shaking out rugs over alleys
a quick slice of smile
been malnourished by years

here where we live in the deep freeze of exile
our will forces seeds to burst
make global warming greenhouse
the secret alleyways
blooming green and green

god is in Ross Dress for Less

god's definitely here. in all these tired-out brown women
looking through racks and racks of what's not lying on the floor:
god comes through for us,
makes us fly and impossibly beautiful

god is the lean finger
that leads us to the red high-heeled
Steve Maddens, the cherry-red stiletto
the Native Tongues hoodie
for $14.99

god is in the woman at the checkout
raising two grandbabies on this job and the DMV, saying,

you look real cute! I remember when I used to dress like that
but since I'm the minister of my church I have to tell you
jesus told ladies they need to cover up more

as she pulls the security tag off my slutty Steve Madden heels
and drops them in the bag without charging me a damn thing

coda:
Sri Lanka, 2009

homeland: Sri Lanka winter 2009

1.
no one gives
two shits
about our country
except us
who gives a shit about some dumb island
with mostly dark folks
pretty beaches   pedophiles
and no damn oil
anywhere

2.
on the A9 highway
shreds of flesh hang in trees
each branch coated with shreds of bombed muscle
ripped from arm   pelvis
delicate toenail
I watch the BBC every fucking day
That's how I hear about things like this
I post the articles on Facebook
No safety zone between our legs
No safety zone in the Vanni   the highway
the refugee camp the INS detention centre
the freezing LondonScarboroughMelbourneStatenIsland
    apartments
No safety zone from either army
No safety zone from the Sinhalese desire for a pure island

jungle trees   rich tamarind soil and flesh
scraped clean and white
like scraping a dinner plate
into the garbage

3.
in Toronto   all colour bleached
from grey concrete and brown brick
by ice salt and snow
brown faces lined early
dry from central heat 'n hours spent
waiting for the bus

In Toronto   in February
no sun for fifteen days in a row
but Tamil families in the co-op
grow curry leaf and green chili
in pots on the balcony and by the stove
in this grey building
all colour stripped by bleach
of salt, ice air and snow

In Toronto   in March
a line of girls like birds bright red and insistent
in the front front of the international women's day march
t-shirts they printed themselves
SRI LANKA IS A FASCIST STATE
in January
and March
45,000 Tamils stop traffic
a bright red, dark brown scar

4.

I get so Sri Lankan for the daughter I haven't even got sperm to
    make yet:

Wear my bangles out. Rock gold not silver.
Memorize the colour list that makes me darker
Find curry leaf in plastic bags at Berkeley Bowl
Insist on practicing my brinjal curry
even when Trader Joes' $1.99 tamales
or Naked Chef pasta are so much easier
Pack hopper mix and Red Label tea in my oversize luggage
Repeat to myself, *no matter what they do to us*
no matter how many of us they kill
as long as the diaspora exists
illankai will never die.

I say I'm trying to write about Sri Lanka

& it's a lie. I want to write sri lanka
instead I take a shower/I check my
voice mail/I make my bed/I
make my bad chicken curry.
Watch The Real News and BBC World Service South Asia/Sri
    Lanka
on internet. Repost. Sleep with someone unworthy of me.

bad dreams later. unsent email. bravest I know
fleeing. quarter million camp concentration resettlement
they don't even know their names
I say I'm trying to write you
old sore
emerald
sister writes: *my darling,*
sister, how are you? when I can sleep,
my dreams are filled
with shattered bodies these days.
How do we survive this?

twelve ways of looking at love cake

it's as heavy as shit
a brown caramel brick
twelve eggs   cashews   pumpkin preserve and
nobody   I mean nobody
knows how it got its name

gramma used to send it every New England winter
aluminum-wrapped   triple-sealed
squatting weird on the sideboard of the dining room we never
    went into
weird like all the things from backhome

grandmas grind cashews
find a foreign or familiar sugar
cream as much richness as can
drizzle honey and rose. all we had
and what came to us:

Portuguese. Arab. Malay. our own
we make it into one dense-ass cake
fat on hips that will travel
packages mailed cross oceans and acres of desire

now I
make my own version
with the nuts I can eat
jaggery chopped off
from the Jamaican grocery

loving this love
this could be mailed across the world
thick 'n built to last
brown preserved by sweet:
watch as I open wide
take a breath
and bite deep

remyth

remyth: children who fly

There are children who learn to fly young. Winging when Bad Things Happen, they have powers of escape, going out the top of their skull when life gets stupid. Because they came down to this planet recent, they are still closer to god, sky, and trees. They go many places out the front of their forehead; the trees, water, cartoons, into a secret language they make up. They have mastered an art that Buddhist scholars take lifetimes to learn.

When they grow up, if they grow up, many things happen. But I dream of an underground army of raped children grown up. Why should all those magical powers go away? What would happen if we all gathered quietly in the hills, some place outside of government surveillance, on lands where wireless and satellites don't go, and all left together? Sent our spirits to Gaza or Killanochi or Kahnesatake, to any place The Thing That Made Us How We Are was happening, and magically reached down? Stopped the computer sequence that launched the rockets, stopped the hand or the penis that reached down and rent a hole in the universe?

Maybe after we would steal away with loved ones and cuddle and fuck, in the bodies that had always been and were once again our own. There would be celebration. Fam. Food. Night. Stars.

early '90s New York femme memory #2
for and after joan nestle

she takes hours to get dressed in almost nothing. the red vintage garter belt found at Love Saves the Day, the basic black mini from the sale table of the Boston Urban Outfitters, Doc Martins, thigh-highs from Marshalls. she puts on makeup for hours, hands shaking making the liquid eyeliner blur. sometimes she gets so turned on by brushing her skin with powder she retreats to the jewelled beaten flat single mattress to jerk off a few times. when she thinks she is pretty enough, she walks out the four-lock door and down the five flights of stairs, and walks the whole of 1994 lower east side New York City in a delirious luxury of time and space. army backpack crammed with books, cigarettes and a bottle of water. the easy May twilight for hours, the city smelling so good, like flowers and piss and cinders and amazement after amazement passing by. stops in the bookstores reading standing up or finding a favourite stoop to smoke for a break.

it's still so new, seeing so many people in city blocks up so late, half the time she doesn't know how to behave. she doesn't know how to say hi to kids hanging out on the stoop, what to do about men following and hissing. where she grew there was nothing but industrial wasteland for miles, with no one else on the streets for hours. It's so precious, that in this city people are allowed to sell books on blankets in the street, hang out in the dry fountain, cover the trains with graffiti and the lampposts with cracked mosaics of junk.

she smells like Night Queen or Egyptian Musk, those sweet oils girls her age buy in a $5 vial. she feels her thighs brushing each other, and she practices. how to stare into the eyes of assholes till they dropped their gaze, or pick my nose and eat it, or scream fuck off, or the hardest: how to truly ignore it and not ever give anything away. private space in this city is small and expensive. so she has to learn to make her private space the six inches of space around her body.

maybe there have always been hermit girls coming into women who dress up for themselves and walk the streets, practise being pretty, smell booze and subway and lilac and cherry blossoms, loll on the richness of the city on the first day of spring. girls becoming women in that narrow sweet space of being eighteen, femme and free. survivor girls who paint on makeup and clothes, the sharp line of a tight miniskirt.

the books say we do this because it is the only way we know how to be beautiful, and that may be true, but there is something else, something about practising hard beauty, with a new room of your own, a door that locks, bare thighs and a glare, practising choosing who or no one to let touch them.

she is exhausted sometimes, when she finally comes back, climbs the five stories and undoes the four locks. she falls back onto the twin mattress and dozes. she has been doing hard work.

there are still days, many days, where her body flies away into grey dust, she strokes it but can't feel a thing. But the days she wraps herself in red silk ribbons like bandages, the days of brown silk thighs brushing, the simple joy of a plum nipple slight and hard under the thin strap of a black tank top, her hair curling out wild years before she has the grown brown girls' lexicon of how to groom and polish—those days, she rubs salve on her thighs, builds a delicate and tough girl skeleton to rise from.

the day I lost my body

the day I lose my body
it's a day like any other and the elements are simple:
1976   a buttercup yellow tract house at 36 wayne
   avenue
a brown baby girl   a white fractured mama
the day I lose my body
my mother loses it
all alone in the house with the baby girl she dreams saves her
she slips   penetrates
and daughter wings free for the first time
like all the winged women of her bloodline
who go up to the golden light
to survive what happens to the body

the day my fourteen-times-great-grandmother loses her body
she smells their ships before they reach the waves
of what I will strain to dream:
Negombo beach in 1517, eighteen generations before my birth
empty of any memory of smashed plastic   tsunami bones
   landmine-scarred metal.
History will say that "friendly relations" between Portuguese
   soldiers and Dharmapala, the King of Kandy
establish a Portuguese monopoly over trade in spice, gems,
   elephants.
"Friendly relations" establish topazes and mestiscos and kaffirs
   and casados,
all the mixed-race children of this penetration.
You know this story

it's every one of our queer-of-colour origin stories
but what we don't always know
is that our origin story
is not just legs ripped open forever
Mestiza mother
is survivor
and she survived
because she dreamed my face

the day we find my body
I am twelve making a lean-to out of trash bags and tomato
    stakes in the woods
I am sixteen making myself come in my bedroom with a chair
    under the doorknob
I am nineteen taking my shirt off at Stonewall 25
I am twenty-one shifting my hips in line at the Canadian border
    checkpoint at 5 am off the Greyhound
twenty-three my hand turning the key in the lock to the first
    apartment all my own
twenty-four shoving all my girl hair in a big hoodie so no one
    can see and stroking my thigh
twenty-six slinging a shaking fibromyalgia leg over an adult
    tricycle riding home from lover's bed
I am thirty-four in yoga class
and my hips still shake   turn in to hide
but I can feel them,
every cell
my body
one thing
that came from the rewriting of Negombo beach and her body
made new

like the language of Creole.
We lost some things forever
and some things
just—
changed

the city of my desire
—after amir rabiyah and li young lee

We own this house. or we don't own it,
but I've lived here forty years now.
we made additions. fixed the hole in the roof. had time, stories
  and bread.
I lived to be an old woman and am still hot
nobody owns anything
but I had time to put down roots
and just live here.
just
live:
We just live here.

In the city of my imagination,
I get to be surprised.
I get to not know
how the story ends.

In the city of my desire
nothing is perfect. oceans rose
people died. people we loved and needed,
they died. not how we wanted them to.
perhaps the water stopped three blocks from my house
because we made sea dikes and magic
and I jog by oil scented salt water every morning.
or I didn't make it and I am a ghost that speaks to my grandchild
who is living in toxic water like Farallon island tiger sharks
still diving and grinning next to cold war nukes dropped thirty
  years ago:
I look at her mutated, beautiful, persistent smile.

In the city of my desire
my diaspora settles like a nervous stomach after a ginger beer
I have family all over the world
in the best tradition of my people,
and I can see them whenever I want.
to where roots stretch dendrons
They are allowed to grow
to flourish
and something new comes
beyond the breaking open of empire
and the IMF bloody wound crust.

The city of my desire
is my body
I spent so long learning to love this crip body
altered by trauma capitalism bled into my mother's stem cells
but things happened:
my parents before dying are accountable for my childhood
old carpet soaked rust belt toxins out of soil
I got to rest as long as I needed
so did everyone else
whose bodies falling apart in the last days of desire
and I limp and jog
I and we the someones
who didn't die

The city in which I adore you
is tricky. complicated.
broken before we breathe it.
all we have. our own genius,
two or three things I know for sure, how genius we are raising
    $5,000 at a house party

how tragic the inside of heart set on fire
it's like arguing over monogamy versus polyamory—
no matter how much I get irritated and compose brilliant
    Scorpio emails
lambasting a lover's dumb ass, I know I can't get married.

The city where I love you
is only this: love storm. broken toxins.
halfassed brilliant solution. oya wind. unknown child.
my feverish tremoring body
 who has time to lie on a couch and write this best poem
of cages crumbled   sea walls holding
drawing the maps crooked bleeding ink
of the city we breathe towards cherished
buoyant dream I reach for
with you, kindred
in this city where we live and desire, now
body brown filled with broken gratitude
breaking bread open breath

Pushcart Prize nominee Leah Lakshmi Piepzna-Samarasinha is a
queer disabled Sri Lankan writer, teacher, and cultural worker. The
author of *Consensual Genocide* and co-editor of *The Revolution
Starts At Home: Confronting Intimate Violence in Activist
Communities*, her work has been widely anthologized. She co-
founded Mangos With Chili, is a lead artist with Sins Invalid, and
teaches with UC Berkeley's June Jordan's Poetry for the People.
In 2010 she was named one of the Feminist Press' 40 Feminists
Under 40 Shaping the Future. She holds an MFA in Creative
Writing from Mills College.